3/97

THE TV FAKE BOOK

W9-ACN-591

Mount Laurel Library
100 Walt Whitman Avenue
Mt. Laurel, N.J. 08054-9539
(609) 234-7319

This publication is not for sale in
the E.C. and/or Australia
or New Zealand.

ISBN 0-7935-3762-2

HAL•LEONARD™
CORPORATION
7777 W. BLUEMOUND RD. P.O. BOX 13819 MILWAUKEE, WI 53213

INDEX BY SONG TITLE

INDEX BY TV SHOW

THEME FROM "THE A TEAM"
from the Television Series

By MIKE POST
and PETE CARPENTER

THE ADDAMS FAMILY THEME
Theme from the TV Show and Movie

Music and Lyrics by
VIC MIZZY

ADAM 12 THEME
from the Television Series

Music by
FRANK COMSTOCK

THEME FROM "ALF"
from the Television Series

Words and Music by
ALF CLAUSEN

BALLAD OF JED CLAMPETT
from the Television Series THE BEVERLY HILLBILLIES

Words and Music by
PAUL HENNING

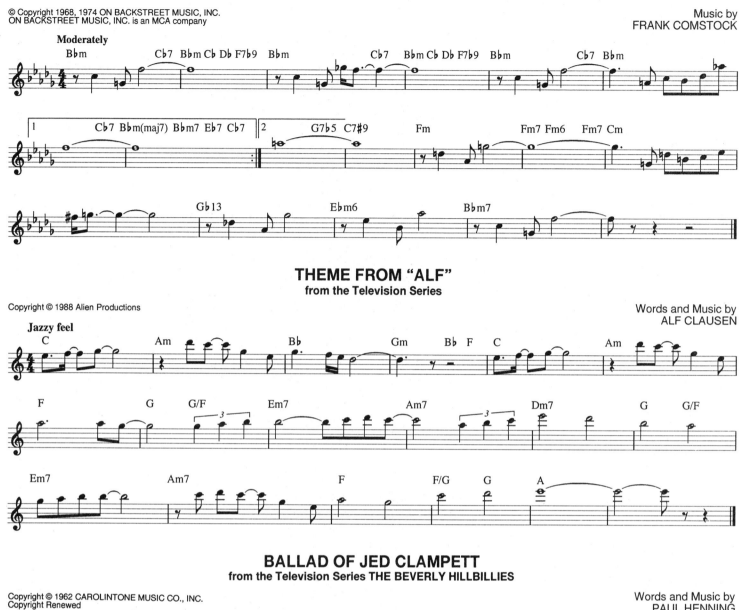

BANDSTAND BOOGIE

from the Television Series AMERICAN BANDSTAND

Words by BARRY MANILOW and BRUCE SUSSMAN
Music by CHARLES ALBERTINE

THEME FROM "BEN CASEY"
from BEN CASEY

By DAVID RAKSIN

THE BALLAD OF DAVY CROCKETT
from Walt Disney's Television Series DAVY CROCKETT

Words by TOM BLACKBURN
Music by GEORGE BRUNS

Born on a moun - tain top in Ten - nes - see, Green - est state in the Land of the Free,
eigh - teen - thir - teen the Creeks up - rose, addin' redskin arrows to the coun - try's woes. Now,
Off through the woods he's a marchin' a - long, makin' up yarns an' a - sing - in' a song,

Raised in the woods so's he knew ev - 'ry tree, kilt him a b'ar when he was on - ly three. Da - vy,
In - jun fightin' is some - thin' he knows, so he shoul - ders his rifle an' off he goes. Da - vy,
itch - in' fer fightin' an' right - in' a wrong, He's ringy as a b'ar an' twict as strong. Da - vy,

Da - vy Crock - ett, King of the wild fron - tier! 2. In 18. When he come home his
Da - vy Crock - ett, the man who don't know fear! heard of Houston an'
Da - vy Crock - ett, the buck - skin buc - ca - neer! fear! land is biggest an' his

pol - i - tick - in' done, The west - ern march had just be - gun, So he packed his gear an' his
Au - stin an' so, To the Texas plains he jest had to go, Where Free - dom was fight - in' an'
land is best, From grass - y plains to the moun - tain crest, He's a - head of us all

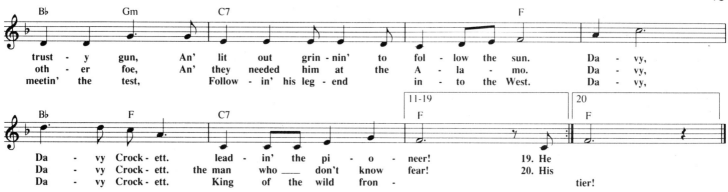

trust - y gun, An' lit out grin - nin' to fol - low the sun. Da - vy,
oth - er foe, An' they needed him at the A - la - mo. Da - vy,
meetin' the test, Follow - in' his leg - end in - to the West. Da - vy,

Da - vy Crock - ett. lead - in' the pi - o - neer! 19. He
Da - vy Crock - ett. the man who ___ don't know fear! 20. His
Da - vy Crock - ett. King of the wild fron - tier!

Additional Lyrics

4. Andy Jackson is our gen'ral's name,
   His reg'lar soldiers we'll put to shame,
   Them redskin varmints us Volunteers'll tame,
   'Cause we got the guns with the sure-fire aim.
   Davy — Davy Crockett,
   The champion of us all!

5. Headed back to war from the ol' home place,
   But Red Stick was leadin' a merry chase,
   Fightin' an' burnin' at a devil's pace
   South to the swamps on the Florida Trace.
   Davy — Davy Crockett,
   Trackin' the redskins down!

6. Fought single-handed through the Injun War
   Till the Creeks was whipped an' peace was in store,
   An' while he was handlin' this risky chore,
   Made hisself a legend for evermore.
   Davy — Davy Crockett,
   King of the wild frontier!

7. He give his word an' he give his hand
   That his Injun friends could keep their land,
   An' the rest of his life he took the stand
   That justice was due every redskin band.
   Davy — Davy Crockett,
   Holdin' his promise dear!

8. Home fer the winter with his family,
   Happy as squirrels in the ol' gum tree,
   Bein' the father he wanted to be,
   Close to his boys as the pod an' the pea.
   Davy — Davy Crockett,
   Holdin' his young 'uns dear!

9. But the ice went out an' the warm winds came
   An' the meltin' snow showed tracks of game,
   An' the flowers of Spring filled the woods with flame,
   An' all of a sudden life got too tame.
   Davy — Davy Crockett,
   Headin' on West again!

10. Off through the woods we're riding' along,
    Makin' up yarns an' singin' a song,
    He's ringy as a b'ar an' twict as strong,
    An' knows he's right 'cause he ain't often wrong.
    Davy — Davy Crockett,
    The man who don't know fear!

11. Lookin' fer a place where the air smells clean,
    Where the trees is tall an' the grass is green,
    Where the fish is fat in an untouched stream,
    An' the teemin' woods is a hunter's dream.
    Davy — Davy Crockett,
    Lookin' fer Paradise!

12. Now he'd lost his love an' his grief was gall,
    In his heart he wanted to leave it all,
    An' lose himself in the forests tall,
    But he answered instead his country's call.
    Davy — Davy Crockett.
    Beginnin' his campaign!

13. Needin' his help they didn't vote blind,
    They put in Davy 'cause he was their kind,
    Sent up to Nashville the best they could find,
    A fightin' spirit an' a thinkin' mind.
    Davy — Davy Crockett,
    Choice of the whole frontier!

14. The votes were counted an' he won hands down,
    So they sent him off to Washin'ton town
    With his best dress suit still his buckskins brown,
    A livin' legend of growin' renown.
    Davy — Davy Crockett,
    The Canebrake Congressman!

15. He went off to Congress an' served a spell,
    Fixin' up the Gover'ment an' laws as well,
    Took over Washin'ton so we heered tell
    An' patched up the crack in the Liberty Bell.
    Davy — Davy Crockett,
    Seein' his duty clear!

16. Him an' his jokes travelled all through the land,
    An' his speeches made him friends to beat the band,
    His politickin' was their favorite brand
    An' everyone wanted to shake his hand.
    Davy — Davy Crockett,
    Helpin' his legend grow!

17. He knew when he spoke he sounded the knell
    Of his hopes for White House an' fame as well,
    But he spoke out strong so hist'ry books tell
    An patched up the crack in the Liberty Bell.
    Davy — Davy Crockett,
    Seein' his duty clear!

BATTLESTAR GALACTICA
Theme from the Universal Television Series BATTLESTAR GALACTICA

By STU PHILLIPS
and GLEN LARSON

THEME FROM "BEWITCHED"
from the Television Series

Words and Music by JACK KELLER
and HOWARD GREENFIELD

THEME FROM "BEAUTY AND THE BEAST"
from the Television Series

Music by
LEE HOLDRIDGE

THE BRADY BUNCH
Theme from the Paramount Television Series THE BRADY BUNCH

Words and Music by SHERWOOD SCHWARTZ
and FRANK DEVOL

BONANZA
Theme from the TV Series

Words and Music by RAY EVANS
and JAY LIVINGSTON

Brightly

We got a right to pick a lit-tle fight, Bo - nan - za!_____ If an - y - one fights an - y - one of us

He's got-ta fight with me! _____ We're not a one to sad-dle up and run, Bo - nan - za!_____

An - y - one of us who starts a lit - tle fuss knows he can count on me! _____ One for four,

Four for one, This we guar - an - tee! We got a right to pick a lit - tle fight, Bo - nan - za! _____

If an - y - one fights an - y - one of us, He's got-ta fight with me! me! _____

BRANDENBURG CONCERTO NO. 2
Featured in the Television Series FIRING LINE

By J.S. BACH

WHERE EVERYBODY KNOWS YOUR NAME
Theme from the Paramount Television Series CHEERS

Words and Music by GARY PORTNOY
and JUDY HART ANGELO

COURTSHIP OF EDDIE'S FATHER
from the Television Series

Words and Music by
HARRY NILSSON

BUBBLES IN THE WINE
Featured in the Television Series THE LAWRENCE WELK SHOW

Words and Music by FRANK LOESSER,
BOB CALAME and LAWRENCE WELK

THEME FROM "STAR TREK: DEEP SPACE NINE"
Theme from the Paramount Television Series STAR TREK: DEEP SPACE NINE

By DENNIS McCARTHY

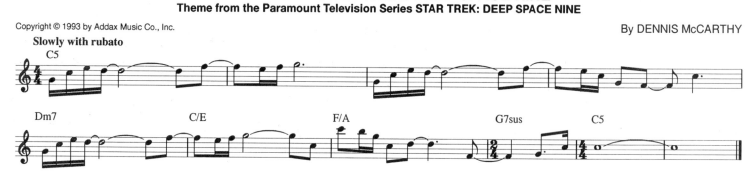

CHIP 'N DALE RESCUE RANGERS THEME SONG
from the Cartoon Television Series

Words and Music by
MARK MUELLER

DALLAS
Theme from the Lorimar Productions, Inc. Television Series

Music by JERROLD IMMEL

CHICO AND THE MAN
from the Television Series

Written by
JOSÉ FELICIANO

THEME FROM "COACH"
from the Television Series

By JOHN MORRIS

DANNY BOY (LONDONDERRY AIR)
Featured in the Television Series THE DANNY THOMAS SHOW

Words by FRED E. WEATHERLY
Music is IRISH TRADITIONAL

1. Oh Dan - ny Boy the pipes the pipes are call - ing___ from glen to glen and down the moun - tain
2. (See additional lyrics)

side _____ The sum - mer's gone and all the ros - es fall - ing 'tis you 'tis

you must go and I must bide. But come ye back when Sum - mer's in the

mea - dow, or when the val - ley's hushed and white with snow. 'Tis I'll be there in

sun - shine or in shad - ow Oh Dan - ny Boy, Oh Dan - ny Boy I love you so. _____

Additional Lyrics

2. And when ye come and all the flowers are dying
If I am dead, as dead I well may be
You'll come and find the place where I am lying
And kneel and say an Ave there for me.

3. And I shall hear tho' soft you tread above me
And all my grave will warmer sweeter be
If you will bend and tell me that you love me
Then I shall sleep in peace until you come to me.

DAY BY DAY
Theme from the Paramount Television Series DAY BY DAY

Words and Music by SAMMY CAHN, AXEL STORDAHL and PAUL WESTON

DEAR JOHN
Theme from the Television Series

Words and Music by JOHN SULLIVAN

DINOSAURS MAIN TITLE
from the Television Series

Music by BRUCE BROUGHTON

DIFFERENT WORLDS
Theme from the Paramount Television Series ANGIE

Words by NORMAN GIMBEL
Music by CHARLES FOX

Moderately, with a strong four beat

Let the time flow, __ let the love grow __ let the rain __ show'r, __ let the rose __ __ flow'r. __ Love, it seeks; __ and love, it finds; __ love, it con - quers; love, __ it binds. We come __ to each oth - er __ from Dif-f'rent Worlds; __ drawn to each oth - er __ by the love in - side __ of us. __ We give to each oth - er __ our Diff'rent Worlds. __ Long as we __ can do it, ____ life, we're gon - na breeze __ right thru it. ____ Let the

D.S. and Fade

DOBIE
from the Television Series DOBIE GILLIS

Lyric by MAX SHULMAN
Music by LIONEL NEWMAN

Do - bie __ wants a lit - tle cu - tie, Do - bie __ wants a lit - tle beau-ty; Do - bie __ wants a gal to call his own. ____ An - y size, an - y style, an - y eyes, an - y smile, an - y Jean, an - y Jane, an - y Joan. Oh, Do - bie __ wants a girl who's dream-y, Do - bie __ wants a girl who's cream-y, Do - bie __ wants a girl to call his own. ____ Is she blond, is she tall, is she dark, is she small, Is she an - y kind - a dream-boat at all; ____ No mat - ter, ____ He's hers and hers a - lone. ____

DONNA REED THEME
from the Television Series

By JACK KELLER
and HOWARD GREENFIELD

DRIVE
Theme from HARDCASTLE & McCORMICK

By MIKE POST
and STEPHEN GEYER

DUCKTALES THEME
from the Cartoon Television Series

Words and Music by
MARK MUELLER

Bright Rock

Life is like a hur-ri-cane _____ here in _____ Duck-burg _ race-cars, la-sers, aer-o-planes. _____
When it seems they're head-ing for _____ the fi-nal _ cur-tain, _ cool de-duc-tion nev-er fails. _____

It's a _____ duck-blur _ might solve a mys-ter-y _ or re-write his-tory. _
That's for _ cer-tain _ the worst of mess-es _____ be-come suc-ces-ses. _

Duck-Tales, oo oo. Ev-'ry day they're out there mak-ing Duck-Tales. Oo oo. Tales of dar-ing

do, bad and good-luck tales. Oo oo. oo. D-d-d-dan-ger, watch be-hind you.

There's a stran-ger out to find you. What to do? Just grab on to some Duck-Tales.

To Coda ⊕

D.S. al Coda

CODA
⊕

Duck-Tales. Oo oo. Ev-'ry day they're out there mak-ing duck-tales. Oo oo. Tales of dar-ing

do, bad and good-luck tales. Oo oo. Not po-ny tales or cot-ton tales, no Duck-Tales. Oo oo.

FALCON CREST
Theme from the Lorimar Productions, Inc. Television Series

Copyright © 1981 by Marilor Music (ASCAP)

Music by BILL CONTI

ENTERTAINMENT TONIGHT
Theme from the Paramount Television Show

Copyright © 1984 by Addax Music Company, Inc.

Music by
MICHAEL MARK

FLAMINGO ROAD
Theme from the Lorimar Productions, Inc. Television Series

Copyright © 1980 by Marilor Music (ASCAP)

Music by GERALD FRIED

EQUALIZER - MAIN TITLE
from the Television Series

By STEWART COPELAND

EVERYONE MAKES MISTAKES
from the Television Series SESAME STREET

Words and Music by
JEFF MOSS

FELIX THE WONDERFUL CAT
from the Television Series

Words and Music by
WINSTON SHARPLES

He's a-maz-ing, he's re-mark-a-ble, He is fear-less, un-be-liev-a-ble. He is su-per doo-per and ex-traor-di-na-ry. ___ He's the kind of guy that keeps you feel-ing mer-ry. ___ Who? ___ Fe-lix the cat, ___ the won-der-ful, won-der-ful cat. ___ When-ev-er he gets in a fix he reach-es in-to his bag of tricks. Fe-lix the cat, ___ the won-der-ful, won-der-ful cat. ___ You'll laugh so much your sides will ache your heart will go pit-a-pat watch-ing Fe-lix the won-der-ful cat.

(MEET) THE FLINTSTONES
from THE FLINTSTONES

Words and Music by W. HANNA,
J. BARBERA and H. CURTIN

Flint-stones, meet the Flint-stones, they're the mod-ern stone age fam-i-
From the town of Bed-rock, they're a place right out of his-to-

ly. ry. Let's ride with the fam-'ly down the street, through the cour-te-sy of Fred's two feet. When you're with the Flint-stones, have a ya ba da ba gay old time. When you're with the Flint-stones, have a ya ba da ba doo time, a ya ba doo time, you'll have a gay old time.

FATHER KNOWS BEST THEME
from the Television Series FATHER KNOWS BEST

By DON FERRIS
and IRVING FRIEDMAN

FRACTURED FAIRY TALES
from ROCKY & BULLWINKLE

By FRANK COMSTOCK

THEME FROM "FRASIER"
from the Paramount Television Series FRASIER

Words by DARRYL PHINNESSEE
Music by BRUCE MILLER

Hey, ba-by, I hear the blues a-call-in' tossed sal-ads and scram-bled eggs, ___ and may-be I

seem a bit con-fused; may-be, but I got you pegged. ___ But I

don't know what to do with those tossed sal-ads and scram-bled eggs. ___ They're call-in'-a

gain.

They're call-in' a - gain. ___

FRAGGLE ROCK THEME
from the Television Series

By PHILIP BALSAM
and DENNIS LEE

THE GROUCH SONG
from the Television Series SESAME STREET

Words and Music by
JEFF MOSS

GEORGE OF THE JUNGLE
from the Television Series

Words and Music by STAN WORTH
and SHELDON ALLMAN

GET SMART
from the Television Series

By IRVING SZATHMARY

GILLETTE LOOK SHARP MARCH
from the Television Commercial

By MAHLON MERRICK

FUNERAL MARCH OF A MARIONETTE
Featured in the Television Series ALFRED HITCHCOCK PRESENTS

By CHARLES GOUNOD

Mysteriously

THEME FROM "THE GREATEST AMERICAN HERO"
from the Television Series

Words by STEPHEN GEYER
Music by MIKE POST

Moderately

Look at what's hap - pened to me; _____ I can't be - lieve _ it my - self.
Just like the light _ of a new _ day, _ it hit me from out _ of the blue, _

Sud - den - ly I'm _ up on top of the world; _ it should have been some - bod - y else. _
break - ing me out _ of the spell I was in, _ mak - ing all of my wish - es come true. _

Be - lieve it or not, _ I'm walk - in' on air. _ I nev - er thought I could feel _ so free. _

Fly - in' a - way _ on a wing _ and a pray'r _ who could _ it be? _

Be - lieve it or not, _ it's just me.

me. _____

HALL OR NOTHING
Theme from the Paramount Television Series THE ARSENIO HALL SHOW

By ARSENIO HALL

HAPPY DAYS
Theme from the Paramount Television Series HAPPY DAYS

Words by NORMAN GIMBEL
Music by CHARLES FOX

THE HANDS OF TIME
Theme from the Screen Gems Television Production BRIAN'S SONG

Words by ALAN and MARILYN BERGMAN
Music by MICHEL LEGRAND

G G/F♯ C/E D/F♯ G G/F♯ C/E D7/F♯ G G/F♯ Em Em/D	If the hands of time were hands that I could hold, I'd keep them warm and in my hands they'd
Csus C D D7 G G/F♯ C/E D/F♯ G G/F♯ Em6	not turn cold. Hand in hand we'd choose the mo-ments that should last; the
Bm Bm7 Em7 A7sus A7 D Dm7	love-ly mo-ments that should have no fu-ture and no past. The sum-mer from the top of the
Dmaj7 Dm7 Am7 F Amaj7	swing, the com-fort in the sound of a lul-la-by, the in-no-cence of leaves in the spring, but
Am7/G D/F♯ C/E Am7/D D G G/F♯ C/E D/F♯ G G/F♯ F6 G7♭9	most of all the mo-ment when love first touched me! All the hap-py days would nev-er learn to fly, un-
Cmaj7 G/B Em7 Am7 D7 G G/F♯ C/E E♭6 G	til the hands of time would choose to wave "good-bye." ____

HAPPY TRAILS
from the Television Series THE ROY ROGERS SHOW

Words and Music by
DALE EVANS

Moderately E♭ Edim7 B♭7	Hap-py Trails to you ____ un-til we meet a-gain. Hap-py
B♭7♯5 E♭	Trails to you, keep smil-in' un-til then. Who
E♭7 A♭ C7	cares a-bout the clouds when we're to-geth-er? Just sing a song and bring the sun-ny
F9 B♭7 E♭ B♭m/D♭ C7 F9 B♭7 E♭	weath-er. Hap-py Trails to you till we meet a-gain.

HARLEM NOCTURNE
Featured in the Television Series MIKE HAMMER

Words by DICK ROGERS
Music by EARLE HAGEN

HAWAII FIVE-O
from the Television Series

By MORT STEVENS

HAWAIIAN EYE
from the Television Series

Words and Music by MACK DAVID
and JERRY LIVINGSTON

HAZEL
Theme from the Television Production HAZEL

Words and Music by HOWARD GREENFIELD
and JACK KELLER

HBO MAIN THEME

By FERDINAND JAY SMITH III

HILL STREET BLUES THEME
from the Television Series

By MIKE POST

HOME IMPROVEMENT
Theme from the T.V. Series

Music by DAN FOLIART

HOGAN'S HEROES MARCH
from the Television Series HOGAN'S HEROES

By JERRY FIELDING

1. He - roes, he - roes, hus - ky men of war, sons of all the he - roes of the war be - fore.
2. All good he - roes, love a good, big fight open up the bomb bays and bright - en up the night

We're all he - roes up to our ear - o's you ask the ques - tions, we make sug - ges - tions,
We ap - plaud the peo - ple who laud us, you pull the ros - es, we punch the nos - es,

that's what we're he - roes for.
that's what we're he - roes for. What's ___ a he - ro do? Well

we're not gon - na tell ya cos we wish we knew. That's why we he - roes are so few. We've got a

slo - gan from Colo - nel Ho - gan and Colo - nel Ho - gan's a he - ro too. Nev - er flinch boys,

nev - er be a - fraid he - roes are not born, boys he - roes all are made. Ask not why boys,

nev - er say die boys, an - swer the call, re - mem - ber we'll all be he - roes for ev - er - more.

HUCKLEBERRY HOUND
from the Cartoon Television Series

Words and Music by BILL HANNA,
JOSEPH BARBERA and HOYT CURTIN

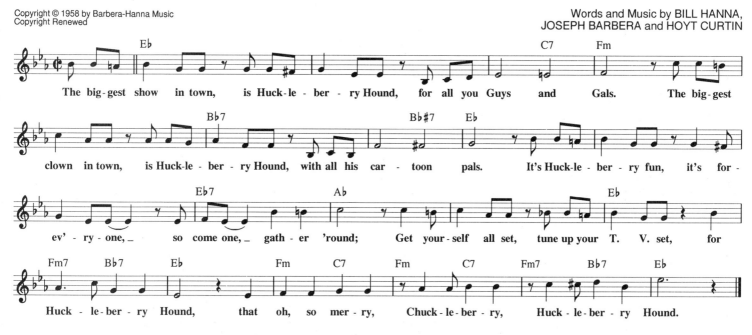

The big - gest show in town, is Huck - le - ber - ry Hound, for all you Guys and Gals. The big - gest

clown in town, is Huck - le - ber - ry Hound, with all his car - toon pals. It's Huck - le - ber - ry fun, it's for -

ev' - ry - one, ___ so come one, ___ gath - er 'round; Get your - self all set, tune up your T. V. set, for

Huck - le - ber - ry Hound, that oh, so mer - ry, Chuck - le - ber - ry, Huck - le - ber - ry Hound.

HOME TO EMILY
Theme from THE BOB NEWHART SHOW

By LORENZO MUSIC
and HENRIETTA MUSIC

I DON'T WANT TO LIVE ON THE MOON
from the Television Series SESAME STREET

Words and Music by
JEFF MOSS

I LOVE LUCY
from the Television Series

Lyrics by HAROLD ADAMSON
Music by ELIOT DANIEL

I love Lu - cy and she loves me, _____ we're as hap - py as
Lu - cy kiss - es like no one can. _____ She's my mis - sus and

two can be. _____ Some - times we quar - rel but then, _____
I'm her man; _____ And

how we love mak - ing up a - gain. _____ life is heav -

- en you see _____ 'cause I love Lu - cy, yes,

I love Lu - cy and Lu - cy _____ loves me. _____

I LOVE TRASH
from the Television Series SESAME STREET

Words and Music by
JEFF MOSS

Oh, ___ I love trash, an - y - thing dirt - y or din - gy or dust - y,

an - y - thing rag - ged or rot - ten or rust - y, _____ oh, I love trash.

I have here a sneak - er that's tat - tered and worn. It's all full of holes, and the lac - es are
I have here some news - pap - er, thir - teen months old, I've wrapped fish in - side it, it's smell - y and
I've a clock that won't work and an old tel - e - phone, a brok - en um - brel - la, a rust - y trom -

torn, a gift from my moth - er the day I was born. I love it be - cause it's trash.
cold. But I would - n't trade it for a big pot of gold. I love it be - cause it's trash.
bone. And I am de - light - ed to call them my own. I love them be - cause they're trash.

Oh, Oh, Oh,

I love, I _____ love trash.

I'M POPEYE THE SAILOR MAN
Theme from the Paramount Cartoon POPEYE THE SAILOR

Words and Music by
SAMMY LERNER

THE INCREDIBLE HULK
Theme from the Universal Television Series INCREDIBLE HULK

By JOE HARNELL

IMAGINE THAT
from the Television Series SESAME STREET

Words and Music by
JEFF MOSS

Moderately

Some-times I im - a - gine that I would like to be a knight in shin - ing ar - mor in a
Some-times I im - a - gine that I would like to be a dar - ing bold ex - plor - er sail - ing
Some-times I im - a - gine that I would like to be a per - son who's named Er - nie who looks

cas - tle by the sea, a knight in shin - ing ar - mor with a prin - cess by my side. I'd
far a - cross the sea, I'd set out on a sail - ing ship to find a dis - tant land. I'd
quite a lot like me, who likes the things that I like and who does the things I do. and I

have a mag - ic feath - er and a horse that I could ride, and the king would say, "Sir Er - nie you're so
gaze a - cross the o - cean with my tel - e - scope in hand, and the cap - tain would say, "Er - nie there's a

hand - some and so brave, please rid us of the drag - on breath - ing fi - re in his cave,"
big storm draw - ing near, you're our fin - est brav - est sail - or, you must grab the wheel and steer,"

and I'd get on my horse and I'd start to ride and I'd trav - el my way through the coun - try side and I'd
and I'd grab the wheel in the wind and rain and I'd steer the ship through the hur - ri - cane and I'd

come at last to the drag - on's cave and I'd yell "Mis-ter drag - on you'd bet - ter be - have!" And the drag - on would be so
guide the ship with a stead - y hand and I'd lead the way toward a brave new land and I'd spy the land ly - ing

(This bar 1st time only)

scared of me that he'd run a - way and the king - dom would be free and I'd tip my hat.
safe and near and I'd cry "Land Ho!" and the crew would cheer

Im - ag - ine that Im - ag - ine that Im - ag - ine that!

1 **(D.C.)** **2 D.C. al Coda** **CODA**

don't have to im - ag - ine 'cause I'm Er - nie, me that's

who and I tip my hat. im - ag - ine that im - ag - ine

that ____ im - ag - ine that!

I'M SO GLAD WE HAD THIS TIME TOGETHER
Carol Burnett's Theme from THE CAROL BURNETT SHOW

© 1967, 1973 Jocar Inc.

By JOE HAMILTON

JEANNIE
Theme from I DREAM OF JEANNIE

© 1966 (Renewed 1994) COLGEMS-EMI MUSIC INC.

By HUGH MONTENEGRO
and BUDDY KAYE

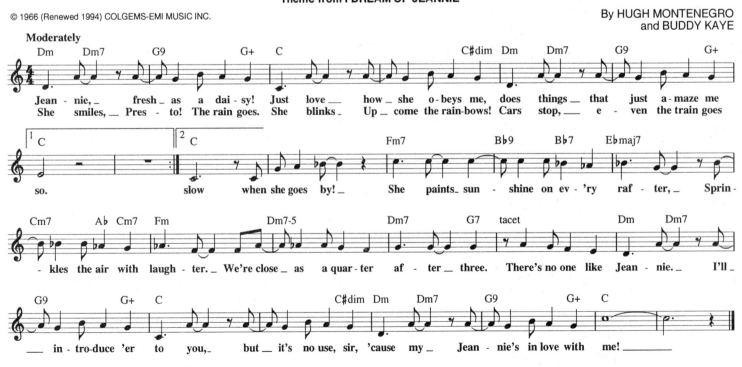

THE IRONSIDE THEME
from the Television Series

By QUINCY JONES

IT'S HOWDY DOODY TIME
Theme from THE HOWDY DOODY SHOW

Words and Music by
EDWARD GEORGE KEAN

KEEP YOUR EYE ON THE SPARROW
from the Television Series BARETTA

Words by MORGAN AMES
Music by DAVE GRUSIN

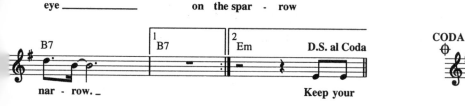

KNOTS LANDING
Theme from the Lorimar Productions, Inc. Television Series

Music by
JERROLD IMMEL

Moderately bright

KOJAK
from the Television Series

By BILLY GOLDENBERG

Moderately

JETSONS MAIN THEME
from THE JETSONS

Words and Music by W. HANNA,
J. BARBERA and H. CURTIN

Lyrics (line 1): Meet George Jet - son! ... Jane, his wife

Lyrics (line 2): Daugh - ter Ju - dy. ... His boy El - roy.

Lyrics (line 3): (Spoken:) And Ro - sy the ro - bot maid. ___

LOVE, AMERICAN STYLE
Theme from the Paramount Television Series LOVE, AMERICAN STYLE

Words and Music by ARNOLD MARGOLIN
and CHARLES FOX

Lyrics:
Love ___ A - mer - i - can Style, _ tru - er than the red, white and blue. ___
Love ___ A - mer - i - can style, _ fre - er than the land of the free. ___

Love ___ A - mer - i - can Style, ___ that's me and you. ___
Love ___ A - mer - i - can Style, ___ that's you and me. ___

And on a star - span - gled night, ___ my love ___
We pledge our love ___ 'neath ___ the same ___ old moon ___

You can rest ___ your head ___ on my shoul - der. ___
But it shines red and white ___ and ___ blue ___ now. ___

While by the dawn's ___ ear - ly light ___ my love ___
And in this land ___ of hopes and dreams, ___ my love ___

I will de - fend ___ your right ___ to try ___
all that I hope ___ for 'tis ___ of thee. ___

Repeat and Fade

Love ___ A - mer - i - can Style, _ fre - er than the land of the free. ___
Love ___ A - mer - i - can Style, _ tru - er than the red, white and blue. ___

THE LIFE AND LEGEND OF WYATT EARP
Theme from the Television Series

Words by HAROLD ADAMSON
Music by HARRY WARREN

I'll tell you a story a real true life story, a tale of the West-ern fron-
he came to Kan-sas to set-tle in Kan-sas, he planned on a peace-a-ble
he was-n't par-tial to be-in' a marsh-all, but fate went and dealt him his
cleaned up the coun-try the old wild west coun-try, he made law and or-der pre-

tier. _____ The West, it was law-less, but one man was flaw-less and
life. _____ Some goods and some chat-tel, a few head of cat-tle, a
hand. _____ While out-laws were loot-in' and kill-in' and shoot-in'! He
vail. _____ And none can de-ny it the le-gend of Wy-att for

his is the sto-ry you'll hear. _____
home and a sweet lov-ing wife. _____
knew that he must take a stand. _____ Wy-att Earp,
ev-er will live on the trail. _____

Wy-att Earp, brave cour-a-geous and bold. _____ Long live his fame and

long live his glo-ry and long may his sto-ry be told. _____ 2. When told. _____
3. Now
4. He

1,2,3

4

THEME FROM "MAGNUM, P.I."
from the Television Series

By MIKE POST
and PETE CARPENTER

Moderately

Repeat and Fade

THE LITTLE HOUSE (ON THE PRAIRIE)
Theme from the TV Series

Music by
DAVID ROSE

LITTLE LULU
from the Cartoon Television Series

Words and Music by
WINSTON SHARPLES

Rac - ing through the pan - try, slid - ing on the floors, rid - ing in the clos - ets, slam - ming all the doors.

How can a la - dy as lit - tle as you, raise such a rum - pus and a hul - la - ba - loo? Lit - tle

Lu - lu, lit - tle Lu - lu with freck - les on your chin, al - ways in and out of trou - ble, but most - ly al - ways in.

Us - ing dad - dy's neck - tie for the tail of your kite, us - ing mom - my's lip - stick for the let - ter you write. Though the

clock says sev - en thir - ty it's real - ly af - ter ten, looks like Lu - lu's been re - pair - ing it a - gain! Though you're

wild as an - y Zu - lu and you're just as hard to tame, Lit - tle Lu - lu I love you, Lu, just the same.

McHALE'S NAVY MARCH
from the Television Series McHALE'S NAVY

Music by ALEX STORDAHL

MAGILLA GORILLA
from the Cartoon Television Series

Words and Music by WILLIAM HANNA
and JOSEPH BARBERA

We've got a go-ril-la for sale, _ Ma-gil-la Go-ril-la for sale. _ Won't you buy 'im take 'im home and try 'im. Go-ril-la for sale. _ See in the win-dow Ma-gil-la Go-ril-la, full of charm and ap-peal, _ hand-some, el-e-gant, in-tel-li-gent, sweet. He's real-ly i-deal. Don't-cha wan-na l'il go-ril-la you can call your own, _ a go-ril-la who'll be with you when you're all a-lone. _ Go-ril-la, Ma-gil-la Go-ril-la for sale. *Spoken:* How much is that go-ril-la in the win-dow? Take our ad-vice, at an-y price a go-ril-la like Ma-gil-la is might-y nice. Go-ril-la, Ma-gil-la Go-ril-la for sale. _

MAJOR DAD
Theme from the Television Series

By ROGER STEINMAN

Spirited march

To Coda

D.S. al Coda

CODA

MacGYVER
Theme from the Paramount T.V. Series MacGYVER

Words and Music by
RANDY EDELMAN

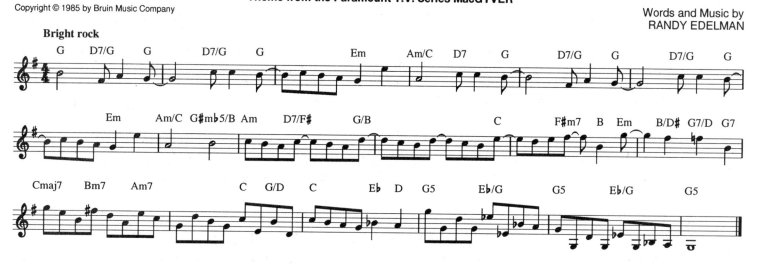

MIAMI VICE
Theme from the Universal Television Series

By JAN HAMMER

MAKING OUR DREAMS COME TRUE
Theme from the Paramount Television Series LAVERNE AND SHIRLEY

Words by NORMAN GIMBEL
Music by CHARLES FOX

MICKEY MOUSE MARCH
from Walt Disney's THE MICKEY MOUSE CLUB

Words and Music by
JIMMIE DODD

MANNIX
Theme from the Paramount Television Series MANNIX

By LALO SCHIFRIN

MARIKO LOVE THEME
from the Paramount T.V. Series SHOGUN

Music by
MAURICE JARRE

THE MASTERPIECE
the T.V. Theme from MASTERPIECE THEATRE

By J.J. MOURET and PAUL PARNES

MISSION: IMPOSSIBLE THEME
from the Paramount Television Series MISSION: IMPOSSIBLE

By LALO SCHIFRIN

THE MOMMIES

from the Paramount T.V. Series THE MOMMIES

Music by RICH EAMES
and SCOTTE GALE

MR. ED

from the Television Series

Words and Music by RAY EVANS
and JAY LIVINGSTON

THEME FROM "THE MONKEES"
from the Television Series

Words and Music by TOMMY BOYCE
and BOBBY HART

MURDER, SHE WROTE
Theme from the Universal Television Series MURDER, SHE WROTE

Music by
JOHN ADDISON

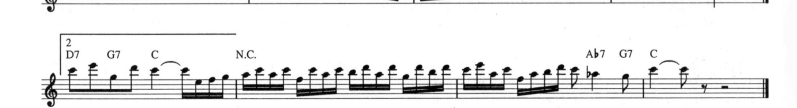

MORK AND MINDY
Theme from the Paramount Television Series MORK AND MINDY

By PERRY BOTKIN, JR.

THE MUPPET SHOW THEME
from the Television Series

By JIM HENSON
and SAM POTTLE

MY GIDGET
Theme from GIDGET

Words and Music by JACK KELLER
and HOWARD GREENFIELD

MYSTERY
Theme from the PBS Television Series

Music by
NORMAND ROGER

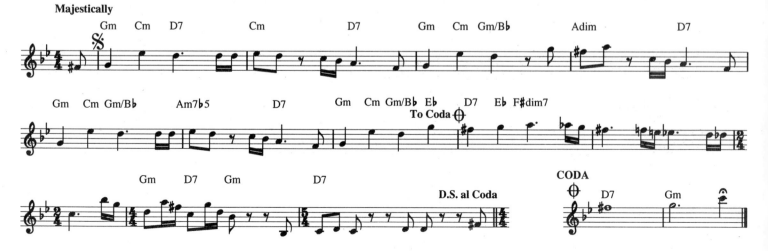

THE MUNSTERS THEME
from the Television Series

By JACK MARSHALL

NADIA'S THEME
from THE YOUNG AND THE RESTLESS

By BARRY DeVORZON
and PERRY BOTKIN, JR.

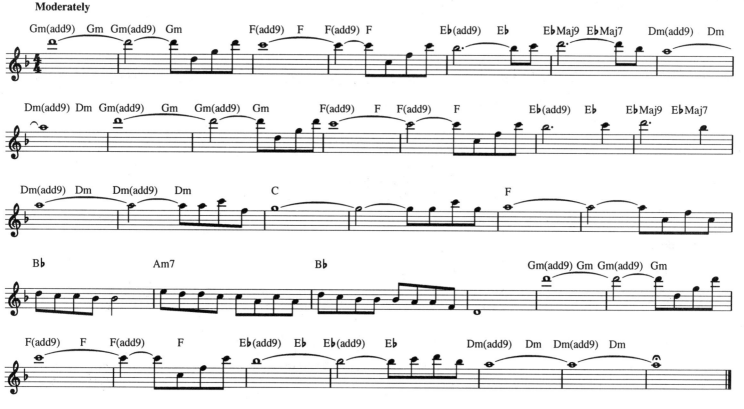

THE NAME OF THE GAME
from the Television Series

By DAVE GRUSIN

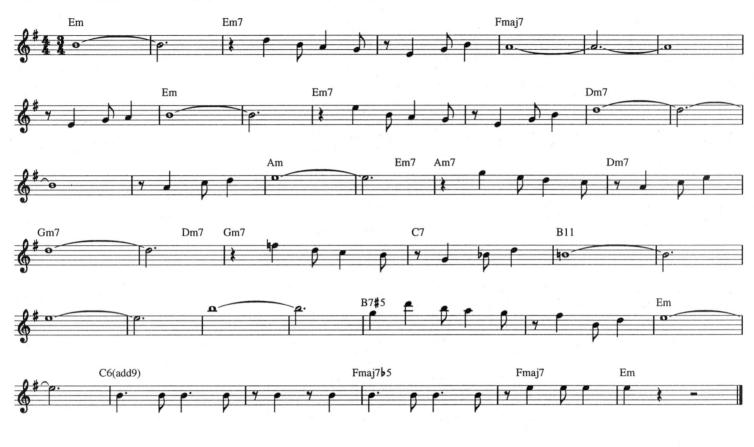

NELSON RIDDLE'S NEW NAKED CITY THEME
from the Television Series

By NELSON RIDDLE

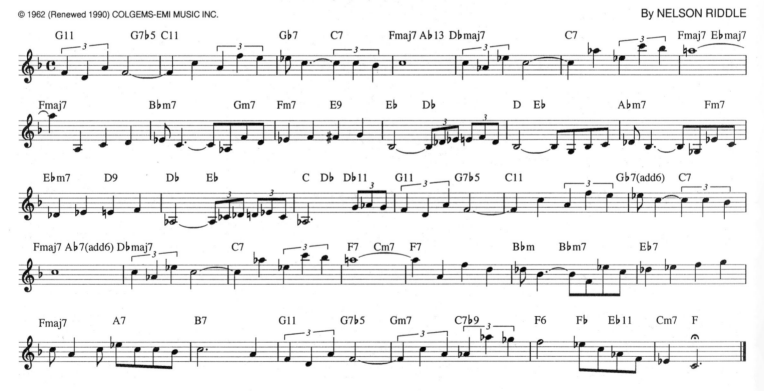

NERO WOLFE
from the Paramount T.V. Series NERO WOLFE

Music by JOHN ADDISON

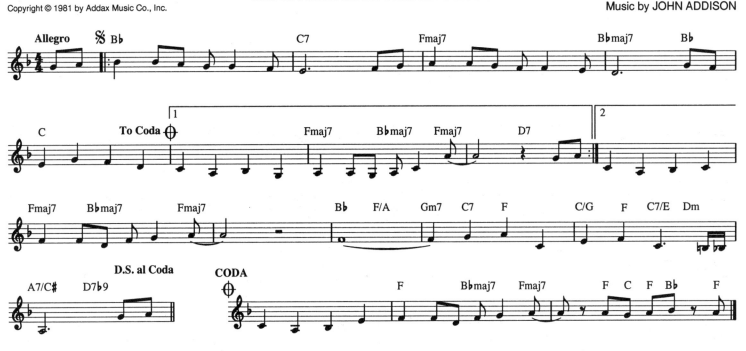

THEME FROM NINTH SYMPHONY
Featured in the Television Series THE HUNTLEY-BRINKLEY REPORT

By LUDWIG van BEETHOVEN

NATIONAL GEOGRAPHIC THEME
from the Television Series

By ELMER BERNSTEIN

NOTHING'S GONNA STOP ME NOW
Theme from PERFECT STRANGERS

Lyrics and Music by JESSE FREDERICK
and BENNETT SALVAY

NORTHERN EXPOSURE (MAIN TITLE)
from the Television Series

By DAVID SCHWARTZ

OCTOPUS BLUES
from the Television Series SESAME STREET

Words and Music by
JEFF MOSS

Slow blues

Well an oc - to - pus' life is - n't eas - y ___ I want to tell you why too many
fish on a date to the mov - ies she said, "Honey put your arms around me tight." I said, "By the
trou - ble with my girl - friend a - mong other things she's an

arms to wave hel - lo with ___ too man - y to wave good - bye." ___ Oh
time I put all my arms a - round you gonna be some - time next Wednes - day night." ___ Oh
octo - pus and she says to me, "Honey, please buy me 8 dia - mond rings." ___ Oh

no, no, no I just don't know which arms to use. ___
no, no, no life is full of tough news. ___
no, no, no life is full of tough news ___

I've got the 1 - 2 - 3 - 4 - 5 - 6 - sev - en 8 blues ___ I took a
I've got

blues ___ I said the 1 - 2 - 3 - 4 - 5 - 6 - sev - en 8 blues, ___ the oc - to - pus blues. ___

THE ODD COUPLE
Theme from the Paramount Television Series THE ODD COUPLE

Words by SAMMY CAHN
Music by NEAL HEFTI

QUINCY
Theme from the Universal Television Series QUINCY

Words and Music by GLEN LARSON
and STU PHILLIPS

ONE FINE FACE
from the Television Series SESAME STREET

Words and Music by
JEFF MOSS

PERRY MASON THEME
from the Television Series

By FRED STEINER

ONE SMALL VOICE
from the Television Series SESAME STREET

Words and Music by
JEFF MOSS

Ev - 'ry song the world sings, each was once un - known. Some - bod - y felt a song in - side and
No tune is too sim - ple. No voice can be wrong. Mu - sic can come from an - y heart and

was-n't a - fraid to sing a - lone. __ If you feel the mu - sic, and you sing out clear and true, then the
an - y-one's voice can lead the song. __ If you feel the mu - sic, and if you be - lieve the words,

world can sing with you. __ Oh __ one small voice can
sing and you'll be heard. __ teach the world a song. Start with one small voice till an - oth - er joins a - long and you'll

feel the mu - sic grow-ing full and sure and strong. One small voice can

teach the world a song. song. __

PUT YOUR DREAMS AWAY (FOR ANOTHER DAY)
Featured in THE FRANK SINATRA SHOW

Lyric by RUTH LOWE
Music by STEPHAN WEISS and PAUL MANN

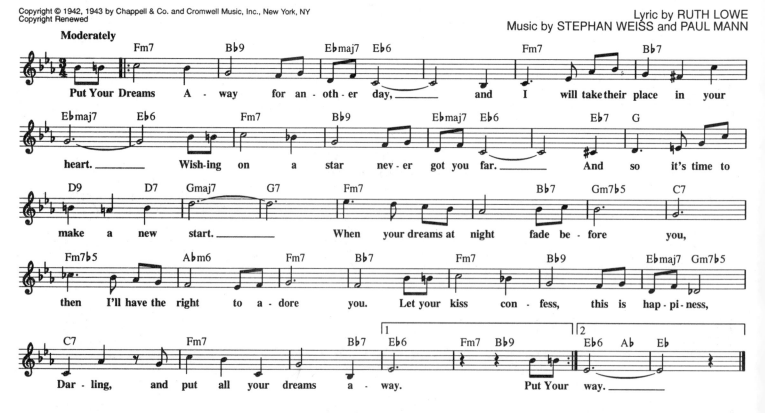

Moderately

Put Your Dreams A - way for an - oth - er day, __ and I will take their place in your

heart. __ Wish-ing on a star nev - er got you far. __ And so it's time to

make a new start. __ When your dreams at night fade be - fore you,

then I'll have the right to a - dore you. Let your kiss con - fess, this is hap - pi - ness,

Dar - ling, and put all your dreams a - way. Put Your way. __

PEOPLE IN YOUR NEIGHBORHOOD
from the Television Series SESAME STREET

Words and Music by
JEFF MOSS

SCOOBY-DOO MAIN TITLE
from the Cartoon Television Series

Words and Music by WILLIAM HANNA,
JOSEPH BARBERA and HOYT S. CURTIN

PETTICOAT JUNCTION
Theme from the Television Series

Lyrics by PAUL HENNING
Music by CURT MASSEY

Come ride the lit-le train that is rol-in' down the tracks at the junc-tion.

For-get a-bout your cares, it is time to re-lax at the junc-tion.

Lot-sa curves, you bet, E-ven more when you

get to the junc-tion, Pet-ti-coat Junc-tion.

There'e a lit-tle ho-tel called the Sha-dy Rest at the junc-tion, It is

run by Kate, come and be her guest at the junc-tion. And

that's Un-cle Joe. He's a-mov-in' kind-a slow at the junc-tion. Pet-ti-coat Junc-tion.

THE NAKED GUN FROM THE FILES OF POLICE SQUAD!
from the Paramount T.V. Series POLICE SQUAD!

Music by IRA NEWBORN

THE REAL McCOYS
from the Television Series

Words and Music by
HARRY RUBY

THE ROCKFORD FILES
Theme from the Universal Television Series THE ROCKFORD FILES

Music by MIKE POST
and PETE CARPENTER

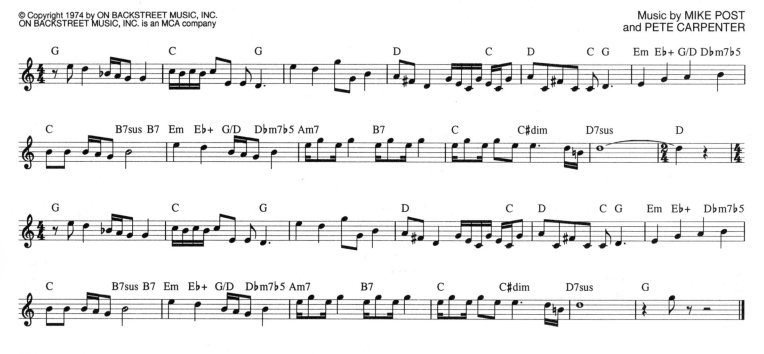

ROBIN HOOD
from the Television Series THE ADVENTURES OF ROBIN HOOD

Words and Music by
CARL SIGMAN

Rob - in Hood, Rob - in Hood, rid - ing thru the glen. Rob - in Hood, Rob - in Hood, with his band of men.

Feared by the bad, loved by the good, Rob - in Hood, Rob - in Hood,

Rob - in Hood.

He called the great - est arch - ers to a tav - ern on the green, the
He came to Sher - wood For - est with a feath - er in his cap, a
With Fri - ar Tuck and Lit - tle John they had a rog - uish look, they

vowed to help the peo - ple of the king
fight - er nev - er look - ing for a fight. They han - dled all the troub - les on the Eng - lish coun - try scene and
His bow was al - ways read - y and he kept his ar - rows sharp. He
did the deed the oth - ers would - n't dare. He cap - tured all the mon - ey that the e - vil sher - iff took, And

still found plen - ty of time to sing. }
used them to fight for what was right. } fair.
res - cued man - y a la - dy

CODA

Rob - in Hood.

THEME FROM "ROUTE 66"
from the Television Series

By NELSON RIDDLE

Moderately

RUBBER DUCKIE
from the Television Series SESAME STREET

Words and Music by
JEFF MOSS

SEATTLE
from the Television Series HERE COME THE BRIDES

Words and Music by ERNIE SHELDON,
JACK KELLER and HUGO MONTENEGRO

ROCKY & BULLWINKLE
from the Cartoon Television Series

By FRANK COMSTOCK

SEAQUEST DSV
from the Television Series

By JOHN DEBNEY

77 SUNSET STRIP
from the Television Series

Words and Music by MACK DAVID
and JERRY LIVINGSTON

Sev-en-ty-sev-en Sun-set Strip, ___ Sev-en-ty-sev-en Sun-set Strip, ___
Sev-en-ty-sev-en Sun-set Strip, ___

A street that wears a fan-cy la-bel, That's glo-ri-fied in song and fa-ble,
You'll meet the high-brow and the hip-ster, The star-let and the pho-ny tip-ster,

The most ex-cit-ing peo-ple pass you by, ___ In-clud-ing a pri-vate eye. ___
You'll find most ev-'ry kind of gal and guy, ___ In-clud-ing a pri-vate eye. ___

SECRET AGENT MAN
from the Television Series

Words and Music by P.F. SLOAN
and STEVE BARRI

Bright rock tempo

There's a man who leads a life of dan-ger; To ev-'ry-one he meets he stays a stran-ger. With ev-'ry move he makes an-oth-er chance he takes. Odds are he won't live to see to-mor-row.

Be-ware of pret-ty fac-es you may find.
sun-nin' on the Riv-i-er-a one day,

A pret-ty face can hide an e-vil mind.
bleed-in' in a Bom-bay al-ley next day.

Ooh, care-ful what you say; Don't give your-self a-way.
Oh, don't let the wrong word slip While kiss-in' per-sua-sive lips.

Odds are you won't live to see to-mor-row.
Odds are you won't live to see to-mor-row.

Se-cret A-gent Man, Se-cret A-gent Man, They've giv-en you a num-ber and tak-en 'way your name. (Look out!) Se-cret A-gent Man, Se-cret A-gent Man, This mys-ter-i-ous life you chose is a dead-ly game.

1.
2. You're game.

Repeat and Fade

THE SMURFS
from THE SMURFS

Words and Music by WILLIAM HANNA,
JOSEPH BARBERA and HOYT CURTIN

La, la, la, la, la, la, sing a hap-py song. La, la, la, la, la, la, smurf the whole day long.

1. sim-ple as could be.
2. La, la, la, la, la, la, smurf a-long with me. La, la, la, la, la, la,

Next time you're feel-ing blue just let a smile be-gin. Hap-py things will come to you so smurf your self a grin.

La, la, la, la, la, la, now you know the tune. La, la, la, la, la, la, you'll be smurf-ing soon.

THE SECRET OF SILENT HILLS
from LASSIE

By WILLIAM LAVA
and CHARLES NEWMAN

One still night a-mong the si-lent hills, I learn'd a se-cret that I will share with you.

In the hush, I heard the whip-poor-wills re-veal The Se-cret Of The Si-lent Hills.

Not a se-cret men scheme and plot for; On-ly true words, we should not for-get.

"Love can cure the world of all its ills." And that's The Se-cret Of The Si-lent Hills.

SOLID GOLD
Theme from the Television Series SOLID GOLD

Words by DEAN PITCHFORD
Music by MICHAEL K. MILLER

The mu-sic has mag-ic, you know you can catch it if you let the
come to dis-cov-er that mu-sic's a lov-er it's heat keeps me

songs take con-trol. The sound starts to glis-ten, the more that you
warm when I'm cold. The beat starts to bend me, the mel-o-dies

lis-ten, and slow-ly it turns in-to gold. Sol-id gold, fill-ing up
send me, and ev-'ry-thing melts in-to gold.

my life with mu-sic. Sol-id gold, put-ting rhy-thm in my soul.

There's a song that's un-reel-ing to fit the way that I'm feel-ing; my head keeps spin-ning to mu-

-sic spin-ning to gold. I've So-lid gold!

SEEMS LIKE OLD TIMES
from ARTHUR GODFREY AND HIS FRIENDS

Lyric and Music by JOHN JACOB LOEB
and CARMEN LOMBARDO

SIMON AND SIMON
from the Television Series

By BARRY DeVORZON
and MICHAEL TOWERS

SONG FROM BUCK ROGERS
Theme from the Universal Television Series BUCK ROGERS

Words and Music by
GLEN LARSON

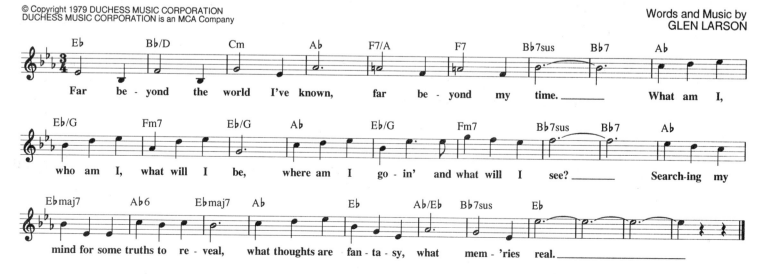

THEME FROM "STAR TREK"

from the Paramount Television Series STAR TREK

Words by GENE RODDENBERRY
Music by ALEXANDER COURAGE

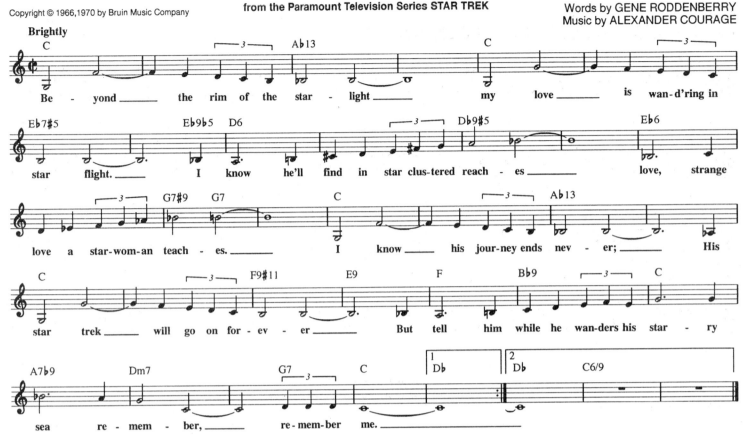

STAR TREK - THE NEXT GENERATION

Theme from the Paramount Television Series STAR TREK - THE NEXT GENERATION

By ALEXANDER COURAGE,
GENE RODDENBERRY and JERRY GOLDSMITH

ST. ELSEWHERE
from the Television Series ST. ELSEWHERE

Music by
DAVE GRUSIN

THEN CAME YOU
from the Paramount T.V. Series WEBSTER

Words by MADELINE SUNSHINE
Music by STEVEN D. NELSON

SUPERMAN
from the Television Series

Words and Music by
LEON KLATZKIN

Moderate March

THIS IS IT
Theme from THE BUGS BUNNY SHOW

Words and Music by MACK DAVID
and JERRY LIVINGSTON

O-ver-ture, __ cur-tain, lights, __ this is it, ____ the night of nights. __ No

more re-hears-ing and nurs-ing a part; __ we know ev-'ry part by heart. ____

O-ver-ture, __ cur-tain, lights, __ this is it, ____ you'll hit the heights. __ And oh, what

heights we'll hit. ____ On with the show, this is it.

To-night what heights we'll hit. ____ On with the show, this is it.

THAT WAS THE WEEK THAT WAS
Theme from the T.V. Series

Words by CARYL BRAHMS and NED SHERRIN
Music by RON GRAINER

That Was The Week That Was, _ it's o - ver, let it go. _ That Was The Week That Was, it start - ed _ 'way _

_ a - bove par, fin - ished 'way be - low.

That Was The Week That Was, _ it's o - ver, let it slide.
That Was The Week That Was, _ it's o - ver, let it go. _

That Was The Week That Was, I took him at _ his word, he took me for a ride Like Mon-day we met _ up at
That Was The Week That Was, I got a _ lot _ to say but noth-ing left to show. On Mon-day he gave _ me no

some-bod-y's pad, _ I don't re - cal much _ but the kiss - ing we had. Like Tues-day was who's day for
beau - ti - ful things, _ on Tues-day no dia - monds, on Wednes-day no rings. _ On Thurs-day he failed _ to add

mak - ing a scene, _ like his day 'cause his way was mood -y and mean. _ Like Wednes-day, Thurs-day, Fri - day I
gold to my stack, _ on Fri - day no mink found its way to my back. _ Sat - ur - day is known to be my

told him to pack _ then I cried all week - end 'cause he did-n't come back. ___
best shop-ping day, _ but I soon found out that he was giv - ing noth-ing a - way. _____

CODA

Oh, what a week that was, That Was The Week _____ That Was. _____

THEME FROM THE "UNTOUCHABLES"
from THE UNTOUCHABLES

By NELSON RIDDLE

Moderately

THIS COULD BE THE START OF SOMETHING

from THE TONIGHT SHOW WITH STEVE ALLEN

Words and Music by STEVE ALLEN

THIRTYSOMETHING (MAIN TITLE THEME)
from the Television Series

By W.G. SNUFFY WALDEN
and STEWART LEVIN

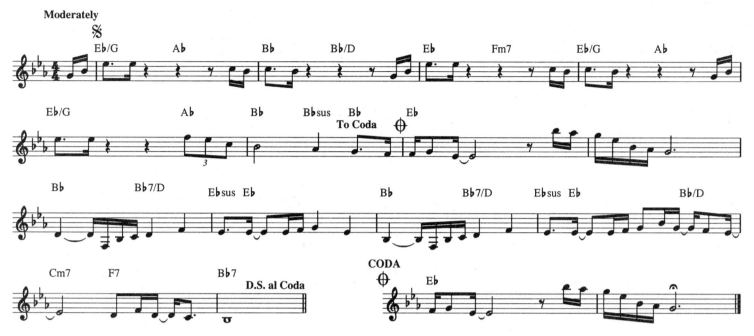

THREE'S COMPANY THEME
from the Television Series

Words by JOE RAPOSO and DON NICHOLL
Music by JOE RAPOSO

TOP CAT
from the Cartoon Television Series

Words and Music by WILLIAM HANNA,
JOSEPH BARBERA and EVELYN TIMMENS

TWILIGHT ZONE
from the Television Series

By MAURIUS CONSTANT

THE WILD WILD WEST THEME
from the Television Series

By RICHARD MARKOWITZ

THE TOY PARADE
Theme to LEAVE IT TO BEAVER

By D. KAHN, M. LENARD
and M. GREENE

VICTORY AT SEA
from the Television Series

By RICHARD RODGERS

TWIN PEAKS THEME
from the Television Series

Words and Music by ANGELO BADALAMENTI
and DAVID LYNCH

(ROLL ALONG) WAGON TRAIN
from WAGON TRAIN

Words by JACK BROOKS
Music by SAMMY FAIN

THE WALTONS
Theme from the Lorimar Productions, Inc. Television Series

Music by
JERRY GOLDSMITH

WHEN YOU WISH UPON A STAR
Featured in THE WONDERFUL WORLD OF DISNEY

Words by NED WASHINGTON
Music by LEIGH HARLINE

WILLIAM TELL OVERTURE

Featured in the T.V. Series THE LONE RANGER

By G. ROSSINI

WINDS OF WAR (LOVE THEME)
from the Paramount Television Mini-Series THE WINDS OF WAR

By BOB COBERT

YAKETY SAX
Featured in the Television Series THE BENNY HILL SHOW

Words and Music by JAMES RICH
and BOOTS RANDOLPH

WINGS
Theme from the Paramount Television Series WINGS

"Sonata in A" by FRANZ SCHUBERT
As Adapted and Arranged by ANTONY COOKE

THEME FROM "ZORRO"
from the Television Series

Words by NORMAN FOSTER
Music by GEORGE BRUNS

WITH A LITTLE HELP FROM MY FRIENDS
Featured in THE WONDER YEARS

Words and Music by JOHN LENNON
and PAUL McCARTNEY

WITHOUT US
Theme from the Paramount Television Series FAMILY TIES

Words and Music by JEFF BARRY
and TOM SCOTT

WON'T YOU BE MY NEIGHBOR?
a/k/a It's A Beautiful Day In This Neighborhood
from MISTER ROGERS' NEIGHBORHOOD

Copyright © 1967 by Fred M. Rogers

Words and Music by
FRED ROGERS

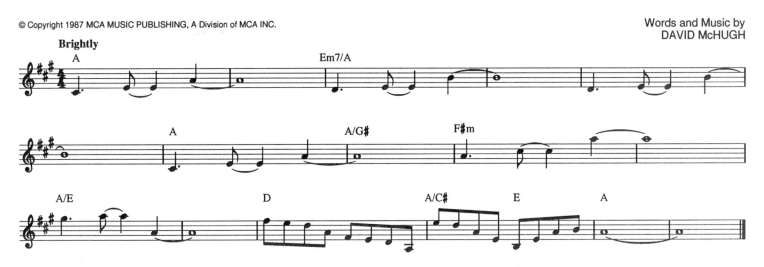

A YEAR IN THE LIFE
Theme from the Universal Television Series A YEAR IN THE LIFE

© Copyright 1987 MCA MUSIC PUBLISHING, A Division of MCA INC.

Words and Music by
DAVID McHUGH

WOODY WOODPECKER
from the Cartoon Television Series

Words and Music by GEORGE TIBBLES
and RAMEY IDRISS

YOGI BEAR SONG
from the Cartoon Television Series

Words and Music by WILLIAM HANNA,
JOSEPH BARBERA and HOYT CURTIN

YOU LOOK AT ME
Theme from the Paramount T.V. Series JOANIE LOVES CHACHI

Words by PAMELA PHILLIPS OLAND and JIM DUNNE
Music by JIM DUNNE

THE ULTIMATE COLLECTION OF
FAKE BOOKS

The Book

The title of this fake book is simple and understated, but the contents speak for themselves. Over 1200 great songs representing every music style imaginable. Special features include plastic-comb binding, a glossary of guitar chord frames, and easy-to-use indexes that enable you to find the precisely perfect song in a matter of seconds. The outstanding song list includes: Achy Breaky Heart • All I Ask Of You • Baby Baby • Baby Elephant Walk • Beauty And The Beast • Body And Soul • Boot Scootin' Boogie • Cat's In The Cradle • Cheers (Theme From) • Don't Be Cruel • Duke Of Earl • Heart And Soul • Here's That Rainy Day • Leaving On A Jet Plane • Memory • Smoke Gets In Your Eyes • Tears In Heaven • and hundreds more!

00240024 C Edition $45.00
00240025 E♭ Edition $45.00
00240026 B♭ Edition $45.00

The Best Fake Book Ever

More than 1000 songs from every genre of music. Includes: American Pie • Boogie Woogie Bugle Boy • Candle In The Wind • Day By Day • Don't Cry For Me Argentina • Dust In The Wind • Girl From Ipanema • God Bless The USA • Imagine • Louie, Louie • Misty • My Way • Somewhere Out There • Wild Thing • and more.

00290239 C Edition $39.95
00240083 B♭ Edition $39.95
00240084 E♭ Edition $39.95

The Ultimate Fake Book

Over 2000 songs! You'll find advertising jingles, international songs, classical music, Christmas melodies, contemporary hits, novelty songs, show tunes, standards, and more! Features 4 unique multi-indexing systems, special guitar chord frames and much, much more!

00240050 C Edition $39.95
00240051 E♭ Edition $39.95
00240052 B♭ Edition $39.95

The Ultimate Jazz Fake Book

Over 625 jazz classics spanning more than nine decades and representing all the styles of jazz. Includes: All The Things You Are • Basin Street Blues • Birdland • Desafinado • A Foggy Day • In The Mood • Take The "A" Train • Yardbird Suite • and many more!

00240079 C Edition $39.95
00240081 E♭ Edition $39.95
00240080 B♭ Edition $39.95

The Ultimate Broadway Fake Book

More than 650 show-stoppers from over 200 shows! Includes: Ain't Misbehavin' • All I Ask Of You • Bewitched • Camelot • Memory • Don't Cry For Me Argentina • Edelweiss • I Dreamed A Dream • If I Were A Rich Man • Oklahoma • People • Send In The Clowns • What I Did For Love • and more.

00240046 $35.00

The Classical Fake Book

An unprecedented, amazingly comprehensive reference of over 650 classical themes and melodies for all classical music lovers. Includes everything from Renaissance music to Vivaldi and Mozart to Mendelssohn. Lyrics in the original language are included when appropriate. Also features a composer "timeline."

00240044 $24.95

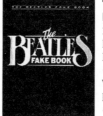

The Beatles Fake Book

200 songs including: All My Loving • And I Love Her • Back In The USSR • Can't Buy Me Love • Day Tripper • Eight Days A Week • Eleanor Rigby • Help! • Here Comes The Sun • Hey Jude • Let It Be • Michelle • Penny Lane • Revolution • Yesterday • and many more.

00240069 $25.00

The Ultimate Country Fake Book – Revised

Over 700 super country hits, including: Achy Breaky Heart • Act Naturally • The Battle Hymn Of Love • Boot Scootin' Boogie • The Chair • Friends In Low Places • Grandpa (Tell Me 'Bout The Good Old Days) • Islands In The Stream • Jambalaya • Love Without End, Amen • No One Else On Earth • Okie From Muskogee • She Believes In Me • Stand By Me • What's Forever For • and more.

00240049 $35.00

Wedding & Love Fake Book

Over 400 classic and contemporary songs, including: All For Love • All I Ask Of You • Anniversary Song • Ave Maria • Can You Feel The Love Tonight • Endless Love • Forever And Ever, Amen • Forever In Love • I Wanna Be Loved • It Could Happen To You • Misty • Saving All My Love • So In Love • Through The Years • Vision Of Love • and more.

00240041 $24.95

The Irving Berlin Fake Book

Over 150 Berlin songs, including: Alexander's Ragtime Band • Always • Blue Skies • Easter Parade • God Bless America • Happy Holiday • Heat Wave • I've Got My Love To Keep Me Warm • Puttin' On The Ritz • There's No Business Like Show Business • White Christmas • and many more.

00240043 $19.95

The Ultimate Pop/Rock Fake Book

Over 475 memorable hits compiled by popular researcher and collector Joel Whitburn. Includes: All Shook Up • Blueberry Hill • Can't Buy Me Love • Endless Love • Every Breath You Take • Happy Together • Hey Jude • Song Sung Blue • Time After Time • The Twist • Your Song • and more!

00240011 $35.00

The Ultimate Christmas Fake Book – Revised

More than 140 holiday tunes, including: Blue Christmas • The Chipmunk Song • Frosty The Snowman • I Saw Mommy Kissing Santa Claus • I'll Be Home For Christmas • Jingle Bells • Rudolph, The Red-Nosed Reindeer • Silent Night • Sleigh Ride • and more!

00240045 $14.95

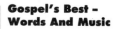

Gospel's Best – Words And Music

The best reference book of gospel music ever compiled! Here's a collection of over 500 of the greatest songs of our time, representing all areas of gospel music.

00240048 $24.95

The Very Best Of Contemporary Christian Words & Music

More than 375 songs written and recorded by America's favorite Christian artists, including Amy Grant, Sandi Paul, Petra, Michael W. Smith, Bill & Gloria Gaither and many more.

00240067 $24.95

FOR MORE INFORMATION, SEE YOUR LOCAL MUSIC DEALER,
OR WRITE TO:

HAL•LEONARD

7777 W. BLUEMOUND RD. P.O. BOX 13819 MILWAUKEE, WI 53213
Prices, contents and availabilty subject to change without notice

0894